D1369903

JENNIFER LAWRENCE

By Audrey Allen

Gareth Stevens
Publishing

Please visit our website, www.garethstevens.com. For a free color catalog of all our high-quality books, call toll free 1-800-542-2595 or fax 1-877-542-2596.

Allen, Audrey.
Jennifer Lawrence / by Audrey Allen.
   p. cm. — (Rising stars)
Includes index.
ISBN 978-1-4339-8978-0 (pbk.)
ISBN 978-1-4339-8979-7 (6-pack)
ISBN 978-1-4339-8977-3 (library binding)
1. Lawrence, Jennifer,—1990—Juvenile literature. 2. Actors—United States—Biography—Juvenile literature. I. Title.
PN2287.L28948 A44 2014
921—d23

First Edition

Published in 2014 by Gareth Stevens Publishing
111 East 14th Street, Suite 349
New York, NY 10003

Copyright © 2014 Gareth Stevens Publishing

Designer: Nick Domiano
Editor: Therese Shea

Photo credits: Cover, p. 1 Ferdaus Shamim/WireImage/Getty Images; p. 5 Dan Kitwood/Getty Images Entertainment/Getty Images; p. 7 Fred Hayes/Getty Images Entertainment/Getty Images; p. 9 Michael Buckner/Getty Images Entertainment/Getty Images; p. 11 Ray Tamarra/FilmMagic/Getty Images; p. 13 Carlos Alvarez/Getty Images Entertainment/Getty Images; p. 15 Vera Anderson/WireImage/Getty Images; p. 17 Frazer Harrison/Getty Images Entertainment/Getty Images; p. 19 Kevork Djansezian/Getty Images Entertainment/Getty Images; p. 21 Murray Close/Moviepix/Getty Images; p. 23 GABRIEL BOUYS/AFP/Getty Images; p. 25 Gustavo Caballero/Getty Images Entertainment/Getty Images; p. 27 Jason Merritt/Getty Images Entertainment/Getty Images; p. 29 Alex Davies/FilmMagic/Getty Images.

Printed in the United States of America

CPSIA compliance information: Batch #CS13GS: For further information contact Gareth Stevens, New York, New York at 1-800-542-2595.

Contents

Following Her Dream 4

Kentucky Born 6

Discovered! 10

The Big Break 16

Action Star 20

What's Next? 28

Timeline 30

For More Information 31

Glossary 32

Index 32

Following Her Dream

Jennifer Lawrence's dream was to be an actor. She followed her dream around the country. Today, she's a star!

Kentucky Born

Jennifer Lawrence was born on August 15, 1990, in Louisville, Kentucky. She liked to play softball and field hockey. She was a cheerleader, too.

Jennifer wanted to be an actor. She began in plays in her school and town. When Jennifer was 14, she went to New York City with her mom.

Discovered!

In New York City, Jennifer tried out
for TV and movie roles. A man on
the street asked to take her picture.
He was a talent scout!

The scout asked Jennifer to stay in New York City for the summer. She acted in commercials. She had a small part in a movie, too.

Jennifer went home to finish high school. In 2007, she moved to Los Angeles, California, to be in a TV show.

The Big Break

In 2010, Jennifer was in a movie called *Winter's Bone*. She learned how to chop wood and even fight for the part!

Jennifer was nominated for a Best Actress Oscar for *Winter's Bone*. She won other awards, too.

Action Star

In 2011, Jennifer was in *X-Men: First Class*. She played Mystique, a girl who could change shape. Jennifer was covered in blue paint!

21

Next, Jennifer got her biggest role yet. She was asked to play Katniss Everdeen in *The Hunger Games*.

Jennifer had to learn archery to play Katniss. *The Hunger Games* was a big hit in 2012. More movies followed.

In 2012, Jennifer was in the scary movie *House at the End of the Street*. In 2013, she won the Best Actress Oscar for *Silver Linings Playbook*.

What's Next?

When Jennifer isn't acting, she likes to paint. She'd like to be a director someday, too. Jennifer is always looking for her next role.

Timeline

1990   Jennifer Lawrence is born in Louisville, Kentucky, on August 15.

2004   Jennifer goes to New York City to try out for TV and movies.

2007   Jennifer moves to Los Angeles, California, to act.

2010   Jennifer stars in *Winter's Bone*.

2011   Jennifer appears in *X-Men: First Class*.

2012   Jennifer has the lead role in *The Hunger Games*.

2012   Jennifer is in *House at the End of the Street*.

2013   Jennifer wins an Oscar for *Silver Linings Playbook*.

For More Information

Books

Aloian, Molly. *Jennifer Lawrence*. New York, NY: Crabtree Publishing Company, 2012.

Orr, Tamra. *Jennifer Lawrence*. Kennett Square, PA: Purple Toad Publishing, 2013.

Tieck, Sarah. *Jennifer Lawrence: Star of the* Hunger Games. Minneapolis, MN: ABDO Publishing, 2013.

Websites

Awards for Jennifer Lawrence

www.imdb.com/name/nm2225369/awards

See what awards Jennifer has won throughout her career.

Jennifer Lawrence

www.people.com/people/jennifer_lawrence/

Read the latest news about Jennifer Lawrence.

Glossary

archery: the activity of shooting with a bow and arrow

award: a prize given for doing something well

commercial: a break during a TV or radio show that tries to sell something

nominate: to suggest someone for an honor

talent scout: someone hired to find skilled people, such as for acting and sports

Index

Best Actress Oscar 18, 26, 30

commercials 12

House at the End of the Street 26, 30

Hunger Games, The 22, 24, 30

Los Angeles, California 14, 30

Louisville, Kentucky 6, 30

movies 10, 12, 16, 24, 26, 30

New York City 8, 10, 12, 30

Silver Linings Playbook 26, 30

TV 10, 14, 30

Winter's Bone 16, 18, 30

X-Men: First Class 20, 30